FLY! 🧡

Fly!
Sheri Block Glantz
Cre8ive Writes, LLC

Published by Cre8ive Writes, LLC, St. Louis, MO
Copyright ©2020 Sheri Block Glantz
All rights reserved.

No part of this publication may be reproduced, stored in a retrieval system, or transmitted in any form or by any means, electronic, mechanical, photocopying, recording, scanning, or otherwise, except as permitted under Section 107 or 108 of the 1976 United States Copyright Act, without prior written permission of the Publisher. Requests to the Publisher for permission should be addressed to Permissions Department, Publishing Company Name and contact information (usually an email address).

Limit of Liability/Disclaimer of Warranty: While the publisher and author have used their best efforts in preparing this book, they make no representations or warranties with respect to the accuracy or completeness of contents of this book and specifically disclaim any implied warranties of merchantability or fitness for a particular purpose. No warranty may be created or extended by sales representatives or written sales materials. The advice and strategies contained herein may not be suitable for your situation. You should consult with a professional where appropriate. Neither the publisher, author, or illustrator shall be liable for any loss of profit or any other commercial damages, including but limited to, special, incidental, consequential, or other damages.

Names, characters, businesses, places, events, and incidents are either the product of the author's/illustrator's imagination or used in a fictitious manner. Any resemblance to actual persons, living or dead, or actual events is purely coincidental.

Sheri Block Glantz
Fly!

ISBN: 978-1-7328130-3-8

Library of Congress Subject Headings:

1. JNF053100 Juvenile Nonfiction/Social Topics/New Experiences
2. YAN029000 Young Adult Nonfiction/Inspirational & Personal Growth
3. FAM 046000 Family & Relationships/Life Stages/General

Copyright, ©2020

ATTENTION CORPORATIONS, UNIVERSITIES, COLLEGES, AND PROFESSIONAL ORGANIZATIONS: Quantity discounts are available on bulk purchases of this book, for educational, gift purposes, or as premiums for increasing magazine subscriptions or renewals. Special books or book excerpts can also be created to fill special needs. For information, please contact Sheri@cre8ivewrites.com.

For my three…
In your grownup faces, I see the children you were, and will forever be, in my eyes.
Fly freely and remember there is always a safe place to land!

If you want to know how much I love and care for you, count the waves.
~ *Kenneth Koch*

*Those early years, now left behind,
 one thought keeps swirling through my mind.*

I'll stand there, and you'll wave goodbye, and, silently, I'll tell you...

My tiny baby, once so new,

the world is big, now so are you.

I wish for you, so many things,

but most of all, for sturdy wings,

With endless skies for you to roam,

you'll never be too far from home.

*Precious child, the world is yours,
filled with hope and open doors.*

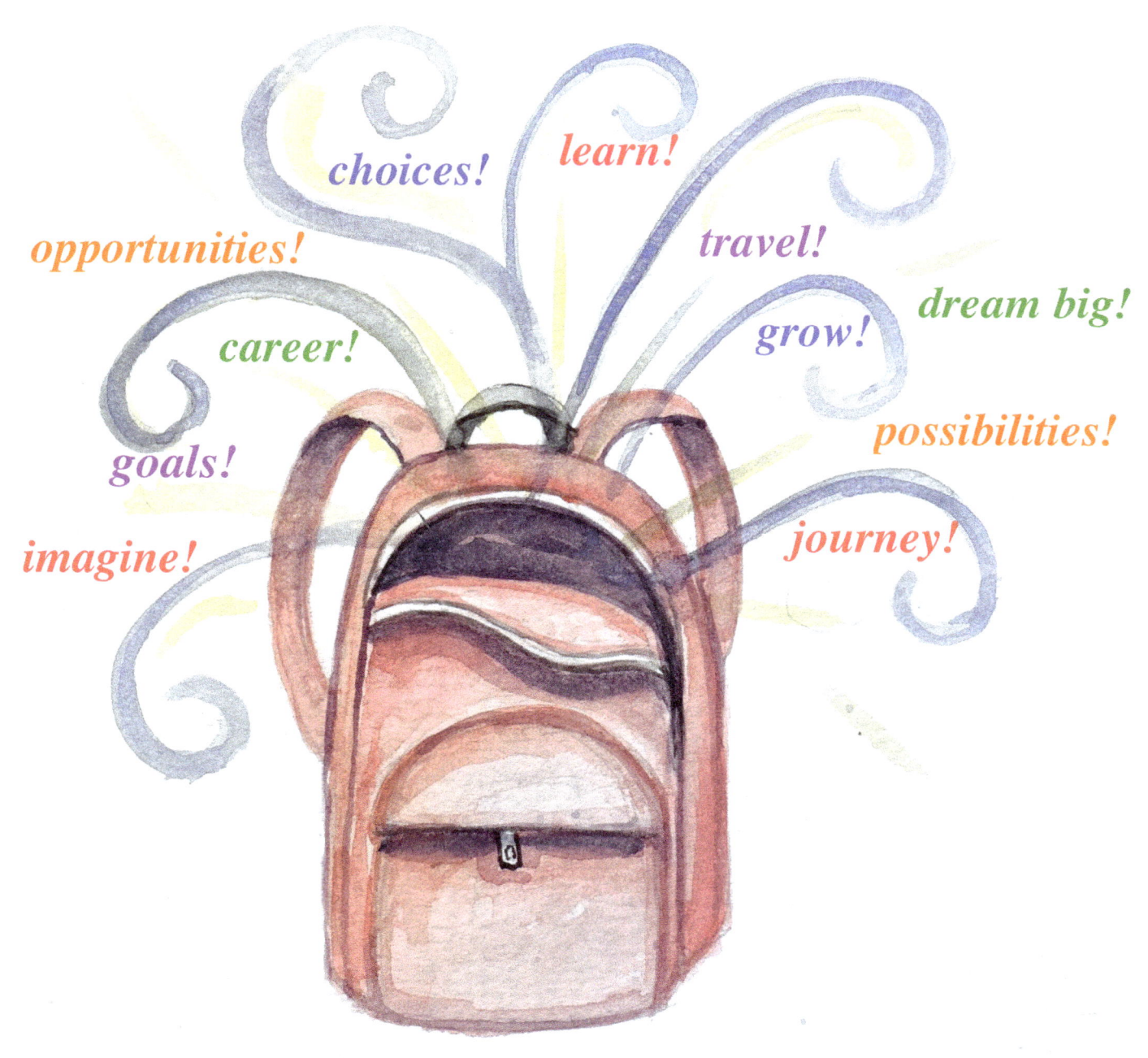

You'd spread your wings. You'd grace the skies with confidence, and realize,

my goal has been to guide and teach that nothing is beyond your reach.

But this time, you will catch my eye,

www.ingramcontent.com/pod-product-compliance
Lightning Source LLC
Chambersburg PA
CBHW081413070526
44583CB00020B/2783